THE Night Sky

BY MARION DANE BAUER
ILLUSTRATED BY JOHN WALLACE

Ready-to-Read

Simon Spotlight
New York   London   Toronto   Sydney   New Delhi

For Eugenie Doyle —M. D. B.

To the children of Vatsalya —J. W.

SIMON SPOTLIGHT
An imprint of Simon & Schuster Children's Publishing Division
1230 Avenue of the Americas, New York, New York 10020
This Simon Spotlight edition June 2023
Text copyright © 2023 by Marion Dane Bauer
Illustrations copyright © 2023 by John Wallace
All rights reserved, including the right of reproduction in whole or in part
in any form.
SIMON SPOTLIGHT, READY-TO-READ, and colophon are registered
trademarks of Simon & Schuster, Inc.
For information about special discounts for bulk purchases, please contact
Simon & Schuster Special Sales at 1-866-506-1949 or
business@simonandschuster.com.
Manufactured in the United States of America 0523 LAK
2 4 6 8 10 9 7 5 3 1
This book has been cataloged by the Library of Congress.
ISBN 978-1-6659-3149-6 (hc)
ISBN 978-1-6659-3148-9 (pbk)
ISBN 978-1-6659-3150-2 (ebook)

Glossary

+ **atmosphere** (say: AT-muh-sfeer): the envelope of gases surrounding Earth.

+ **constellations** (say: kon-stuh-LAY-shuhns): groups of stars forming recognizable patterns. Different people at different times in history have used their own favorite stories to find images in the stars.

+ **meteors** (say: MEE-tee-ors): dust or rocks from outer space that burn when they enter Earth's atmosphere, appearing to us as streaks of light.

+ **northern lights** (aurora borealis) (say: uh-RORE-uh bore-ee-A-luss): a display of colorful lights in the sky seen mostly in the far north. The lights are caused by solar wind. They occur near the South Pole, too, and then are called southern lights (aurora australis).

+ **Perseid meteor shower** (say: PUR-see-ud MEE-tee-or SHAU-er): a heavier-than-usual display of meteors that appears in mid-August. The name comes from the fact that the meteors seem to radiate from a point in a constellation known as Perseus.

+ **telescope** (say: TEH-luh-skohp): an instrument designed to make distant objects appear nearer.

Note to readers: Some of these words may have more than one definition. The definitions above match how these words are used in this book.

Did you know that stars shine day and night?

We do not see stars
in the daytime
because the star
closest to us, our sun,
outshines them all.

To see the night sky
in all its glory,
leave city lights behind.

Wait for your eyes
to get used to the dark.
Then look up.
Wow!

On most nights,
you can see our moon first.
Because it is so close,
it seems larger
than anything else.

The moon's face changes every night. Sometimes it is round.

Sometimes it is just a sliver.

Then there are all
those twinkling stars.

They twinkle because their light bounces and bumps through our **atmosphere** to reach us.

Atmosphere

Humans have always made connect-the-dots pictures with the stars.

We call those pictures **constellations**.

The ancient Greeks imagined the hunter Orion in this group of stars.

In the same stars,
the Navajo saw the
First Slender One,
a warrior protecting
his people.

Planets are closer than stars, so they do not twinkle. They look like flat disks of light.

Mercury, Venus,
Mars, Jupiter,
and Saturn can all be
seen without a **telescope**.

Have you ever seen
a falling star?

Falling stars are not really stars. They are **meteors**.

Meteors are made up of rocks from outer space.

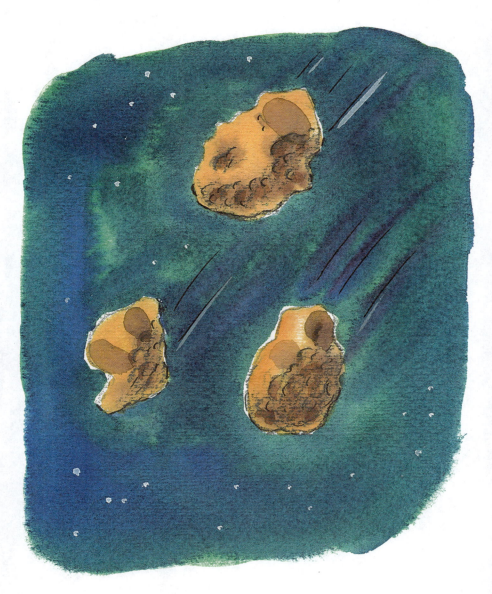

Most burn up before
they reach the ground.
But if they do land,
they are called meteorites.

In August during the **Perseid meteor shower,** you might see up to one hundred meteors in an hour.

Many stories are told about the **northern lights**. In China people saw a battle between dragons in those lights.

In Finland the lights are foxes brushing snowflakes into the sky with their tails.

Whatever story they tell, these dancing lights are spectacular!

Do you want to glimpse our fascinating universe? Just look at the night sky.

Interesting Facts

✦ About nine thousand stars are visible to the bare eye, but only half are visible from one place. That's because half of Earth is always in sunlight, which means that all the stars aren't visible at the same time.

✦ Ancient sailors navigated by measuring the position of certain stars to the horizon. Modern sailors and even airplane pilots can navigate by the stars too.

✦ The North Star stands almost directly over the North Pole, so it can be used to find north. It holds nearly still in the sky while all the other stars appear to move around it.

✦ The Big Dipper is a favorite image in the sky. It is called an asterism, not a constellation, because it is part of a bigger constellation, Ursa Major (Great Bear).

✦ Big telescopes on the ground use lasers and mirrors to take the twinkle out of starlight so astronomers can see the stars more clearly.

✦ In 1990 the United States guided a powerful telescope, Hubble, into orbit 332 miles above Earth's surface. For more than thirty years Hubble has sent back images that have taught us much about our universe.

✦ In 2021 the James Webb Space Telescope was launched into orbit. It traveled a million miles from Earth. The Webb is one hundred times more powerful than the Hubble and can see much farther into space, revealing a universe we have only been able to imagine before now.